Look at the colours of Life

TALKING CUB
Published by Speaking Tiger Books LLP
125A, Ground Floor, Shahpur Jat
New Delhi 110049

First published in paperback in Talking Cub by Speaking Tiger Books in 2023

ISBN: 978-93-5447-398-2
eISBN: 978-93-5447-399-9

10 9 8 7 6 5 4 3 2 1

Printed at :- Pragati Printers, Nariana Inds Area Phase-1

Look at the COLOURS of Life

RUSKIN BOND

Illustrated by Ambika Karandikar

talking CUB
An Imprint of Speaking Tiger Books

Colours are everywhere,

Bright blue the sky,

Dark green the forest

And light the fresh grass

Bright yellow the lights
From a train sweeping past

The Flame trees glow
At this time of year,
The mangoes burn bright
As the monsoon draws near.

A favourite colour of mine
Is the pink of the candyfloss man

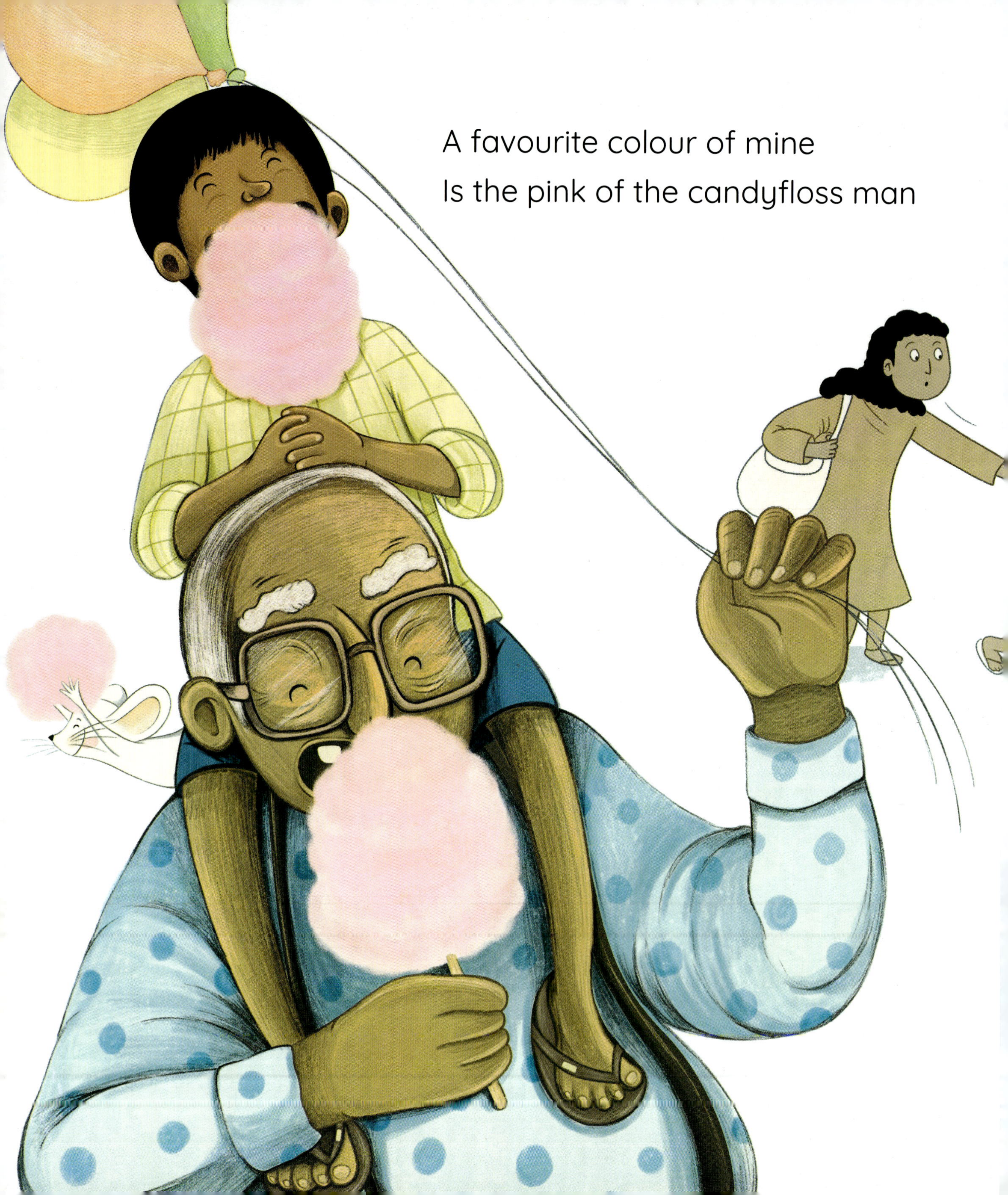

As he comes down
the dusty road,
Calling his wares,
And the balloon-man
soon follows,
Selling his floating
bright colours.

It's early summer
And the roses blush
In the dew-drenched dawn,

And poppies sway red and white
In the invisible breeze.

Only the wind has no colour:

But if you look carefully

You will see it teasing
The colour out of the leaves.

And the rain has no colour
But it turns the bronzed grass
To emerald green,

And gives a golden sheen
To the drenched sunflower.

Look for the colours of life—
They are everywhere,
Even in your dreams.

Ruskin Bond is the author of numerous novellas, short-story collections and non-fiction books, many of them classics. Among them are *When I Was a Boy*, *Lone Fox Dancing*, *The Room on the Roof*, *A Flight of Pigeons*, and *A Book of Simple Living*. He received the Sahitya Akademi Award in 1993, the Padma Shri in 1999 and the Padma Bhushan in 2014.

Ambika Karandikar is an illustrator, Bharatnatyam dancer and official garden ambassador to butterflies, birds and a team of cats. She has been drawing ever since she can remember and loves to illustrate for children through different mediums.

More poetry books by

Ruskin Bond

Illustration by Barkha Lohia from the book *A Tree of My Own*

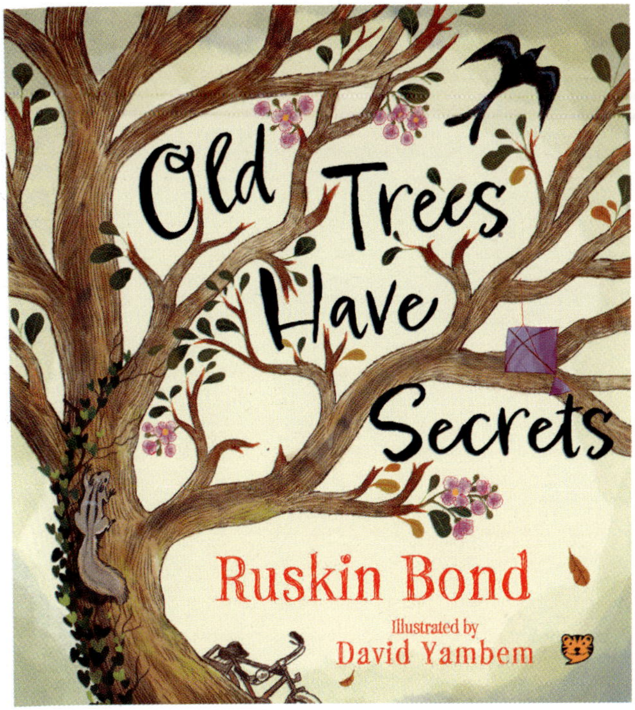
Old Trees Have Secrets
Ruskin Bond
Illustrated by
David Yambem

Granny's Tree-climbing
Ruskin Bond
Illustrated by Ekta Bharti

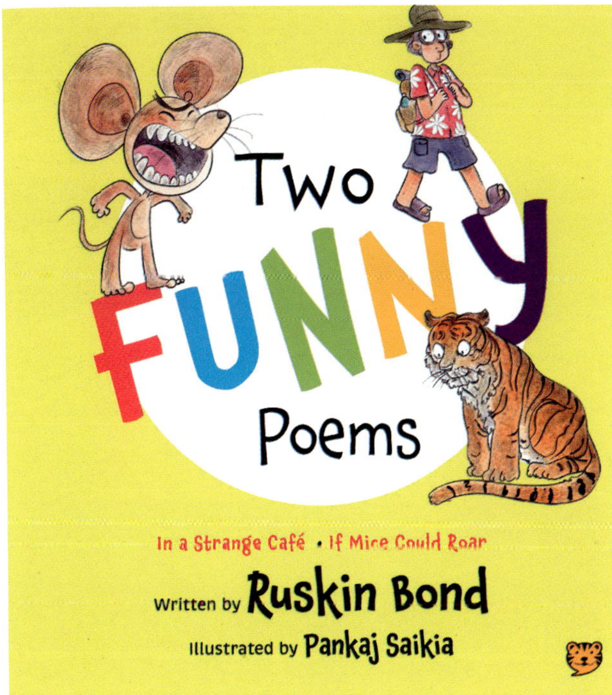
Two FUNNY Poems
In a Strange Café • If Mice Could Roar
Written by Ruskin Bond
Illustrated by Pankaj Saikia

Ruskin Bond
a tree of my Own
Illustrated by
Barkha lohia

The **FUN** never stops with these poetry books from Talking Cub!